A WORD FOR YOUR WOMB

A COLLECTION OF PSALMS, PRAYERS, POETRY, AND PRAISE

ALICIA L. WATERS

WestBow
PRESS
A DIVISION OF THOMAS NELSON

Scripture taken from the New King James Version. Copyright 1979, 1980,
1982 by Thomas Nelson, inc. Used by permission. All rights reserved.

WestBow Press books may be ordered through booksellers or by contacting:

WestBow Press
A Division of Thomas Nelson
1663 Liberty Drive
Bloomington, IN 47403
www.westbowpress.com
1-(866) 928-1240

ISBN: 978-1-4497-1866-4 (sc)

Library of Congress Control Number: 2011930950

Printed in the United States of America

WestBow Press rev. date: 07/19/2011

The book is dedicated to you…Push!

Lord, let my life be a reflection of Your
Truth as I walk in You...the Light.

CONTENTS

POETRY | 43

PRAISE | 65

ACKNOWLEDGEMENTS

Lord, thank You for Your unconditional love. I am grateful for Your Living Water that flows through me, I shall never thirst again. Ron, I love you so much. Thank you for being who you are. Asha and Aaron, you are my biggest fans, thank you for making me smile. I love you more than more. My amazing mother, Estelle McCreary, you are simply the best. Carrie Waters, I love you more than you know.

To LaVender Williams (Momsweb), Margarita Hudson, Rhonda Gould, Ken & Patrice Barnes, Bruce & Anita Hemphill, Ervin & Carrie McWilson, Lonnie & LaTonya Wesley, Carney & Cheryl Anderson, Margie Lucas, Darryl & Kaaren Shaw, Rhonda Gillard, Florence Windon, and Taneka Harris...thank you. You all have encouraged me, inspired me, blessed me...I love you all!

INTRODUCTION

The Womb…the birthing place…the beginning.

God's will is carried out through the works of those who believe His Word and are obedient to His instruction. As Believers, we are equipped with the tools necessary to fulfill God's purpose, His perfect will for our lives. Our purpose begins in the womb. The womb is the birthing place where our purpose is developed and nurtured.

The womb is our inner part that holds the work that God placed in us to get out of us in order to edify the Body of Christ. An amazing process takes place in the womb: gifts and talents are developed with the life that God supplies, growth takes place as we provide nutrition to the life inside with the Word of God, and God, Our Father in Heaven, is glorified.

Realizing our purpose and acting on it requires faith: faith to PUSH through the trials of life, faith to trust God and every aspect of His plan, and faith to go beyond the limits of our minds. While we all experience pain, setbacks, letdowns, and other mistakes or misfortunes, these challenges do not have to be our end result. We are more than conquerors. This book encourages you to push past the pain from previous disappointments and give birth to something greater…your purpose.

Being confident of this that He who began a good work in you will carry it until…Philippians 1:6

Psalms...

sacred songs, expressions of love,
adoration, and thanksgiving

EACH DAY I RISE

Each day I rise to a day I've never seen
before and a day I'll never see again

Each day I rise thanking God...Amen

Each day I rise with a desire to live a better life today

Each day I rise thanking God just for being the Way

Each day I rise appreciating the air that I breathe

Each day I rise seeking the Lord, aiming to please

Each day I rise filled with His joy, peace, and love

Each day I rise giving thanks to God, in Heaven above

Each day I rise realizing that tomorrow is not guaranteed

Each day I rise asking for help on this journey, I plead

Each day I rise ready to see what the Lord has in store for me

Each day I rise looking forward to new
mercies, new opportunities

Each day I rise with a praise on my
lips and a dance in my step

Each day I rise grateful for my life, He so mercifully kept

Each day I rise, I realize that I'm alive...each day I rise.

This is the day the Lord has made; We will rejoice and be glad in it.
Psalm 118:24 NKJV

SUPER NATURAL

He is able to do exceedingly, abundantly
above all that I can ask or think…

He knows the end from the beginning,
while others are on the brink…

He is the Creator, Master of the Universe,
all power is in His hands…

He spoke the world into existence, the earth
and sky appeared at His command…

He is the ultimate Healer, with power that cannot be beat…

Understanding exactly who He is, keeps me at His feet…

Everything I need He is, His promises do not expire…

He fulfills my every need and knows my every desire…

He is the Master Cleanser, able to
clean from the inside out…

He is a God of restoration, removing all fear and doubt…

He is a promise-keeper; dependable, faithful is His Name…

He is never changing, always consistent…yesterday,
today, forevermore, always the same.

For He spoke, and it was done; He commanded, and it stood fast.
Psalm 33:9 NKJV

DANCE

Is it like fire shut up in your bone?
Dance!
Do you feel the need to shed your clothes?
Dance!
Thinking of His goodness, you're moved to lift your hands
Dance!
You're glad He gave you yet another chance
Dance!
You skip to the beat of your heart
Dance!
You're grateful He gave you a new start
Dance!
Once blinded, you now see your way
Dance!
You're just thankful for another day
Dance!

Praise Him with the timbrel and dance.
Psalm 150:4 NKJV

OVERWHELMED

I see no way out
No way to breakthrough
I'm broken and overwhelmed
What am I to do?
Carrying the weight of the world
As if power is in my hands
Release it, let it go
Give it to the One who can.

Commit your way to the Lord, Trust also in Him, And He shall bring it to pass.
Psalm 37:5 NKJV

MY EVERYTHING

You are the fresh wind in the heat of the day
The calm in the midst of any storm
You drive all pain away
When I feel I can't go on
In silence, You are the still that calms all my fears
In sadness, You are the joy that dries all my tears
In despair, You are the hope that my soul holds on to
Your Word is the only Way that always sees me through
The Holy One, Source of All, You are the Matchless King
Omnipotent, Omnipresent, Lord, You are my everything.

Behold, God is my helper; The Lord is with those who uphold my life.
Psalm 54:4 NKJV

IN THE MEANTIME

In the meantime, the in between time, where I patiently wait
An humble heart, an opened mind, the answer I anticipate
In the meantime, the in between time, where I seek His face
Faith no fear, I know He's near, I'm in the safest place

In the meantime, the in between time,
where I cast all my cares

My challenges and trials, it's all worthwhile, my burdens I know He bears

In the meantime, the in between time,
no time for compromise

He knows the end, I can depend on Him, I'm not that wise

In the meantime, the in between time,
I can be real or I can be phony

I choose to stand strong, it won't be too
long, this builds my testimony

In the meantime, the in between time,
on His promises I will stand

I've tried, I know, it's time to let go
and trust The One who can.

*Wait on the Lord; Be of good courage. And He shall
strengthen your heart; Wait I say on the Lord!*

Psalm 27:14 NKJV

Trust in the **presence** of God. Trust in the **promises** of God. Trust in the **power** of God...have **FAITH**.

Push...

Now faith is the substance of things hoped for, the evidence of things not seen.

Hebrews 11:1 NKJV

I AM

I am a woman of God, I am a woman of
faith, I cannot be swayed otherwise

The Regulator, The Comforter, The Holy
Spirit just won't let me compromise

I am strong, I am secure, I am humbled at His feet

I am triumphant, walking in victory…no despair, no defeat

I am blessed and highly favored, living an abundant life

I am running and I won't quit…
no room for misery and strife

I am trusting in His Word, standing on His promises,
seeking everything He has in store for me

I am, I am, I am striving to be the
woman He's called me to be.

I will praise You, for I am fearfully and wonderfully made;
Psalms 139:14 NKJV

Each day I make a conscious effort to hear the voice of God as He directs me in my writing. Attention to details and the obvious gives me the inspiration to express my thoughts and feelings about my Lord and His faithfulness. Today my daughter Asha and I were having lunch when God spoke to me about a concept for a piece to write…"what if". As I was typing each word into my Blackberry, I was overcome with emotion as I listened to God's voice…word after word I listened, I typed. I love it when I'm in a position where I can hear Him without distractions (even in a crowded place).

In my haste to complete the piece I accidentally deleted the work. Tears immediately came to my eyes as I stared at a blank screen. I sat there crushed remembering how the words flowed and how honored I was to be used by God. Refusing to move on or just sit there and cry I began to pray: "God if You gave it to me before, I know You will give it to me again". Sure enough the words began to flow like water from a stream. Hallelujah…God is an awesome God! I completed the piece in a matter of minutes and immediately saved the draft. As I embraced His presence, I took pleasure in knowing that you can hear from God, if you take time to listen.

WHAT IF...

What if there was no sun to shine or no rain to fall...
What if there was no moon at night when darkness calls...
What if there were no waters to fill the rivers and streams...

What if there were no clouds in the
sky or dreams to dream...

What if when we called no one replied...

What if no one was there to wipe the tears we cried...

What if there was no grace, no mercy,
no forgiveness for sin...

What if there was no Holy Spirit to remind
us of Truth, time and time again...

What if there was no protection from all hurt and harm...

What if there was no provision when
circumstances cause us alarm...

What if we had to rely on our limited
knowledge and superficial ideals...

What if God's presence could not be found
and His love we could not feel...

But He is alive and present and all power yes, is His...

We can rest assured and find comfort in
knowing that "what if" is not what is.

God is our refuge and strength, A very present help in trouble.
Psalm 46:1 NKJV

MY SOUL SAYS YES

O Lord, I hear You calling

I surrender, my soul says yes

I accept You as my Savior

To be my Lord

O yes, yes, yes

Come into my life

And make me over

I need Your spirit

To take control

I surrender my all to You

Yes to Your will

Yes to Your way

Create in me a clean heart, O God, And
renew a steadfast spirit within me.

Psalm 51:10 NKJV

VERTICAL PRAISE

From me to You, Lord I offer my praise
With an humbled heart and lifted hands…so many ways
To express my appreciation for Your love
For Your passion for Your people is far above
Any gift any man could ever give
You gave your life that I might live
Free from bondage and the penalty of sin
My heart is open so You can come in
Breathe in me, live in me
Lord, have Your way
Lord let Your spirit take residence…today
Your love, Your peace, Your joy complete my life
I live for You, dear Jesus, I need You to
Accept this praise as I honor You
Without You Lord, what would I do?

But You are holy, Enthroned in the praises of Israel.
Psalm 22:3 NKJV

NIGHT

It's dark and I feel all alone
Don't know exactly what to do
Seems all hope is gone
Not sure if I'll make it through

Cold and empty
Desperate and in despair
I need resolution to this situation
I need to know You're there

Yes, I know…the Word says trouble won't last always
But I'm so broken right now
I can't even offer up a praise

Tears flowing as fear enters my mind
Faith do your thing… it's your time

Who knew that the night would last this long?
Holy Ghost please
Give me a Word or give me a song

All I know is that tomorrow has got to be a better day
…while I'm complaining I forgot to pray

….Amen, it's morning.

…Weeping may endure for a night, But joy comes in the morning.
Psalm 30:5 NKJV

GOD GOOD

This morning when I rose...
God Good
Realized that I was closed in my right mind...
God Good
I've got the ability of all my limbs...
God Good
In fact, I'm feeling mighty fine...
God Good
I've got food, water, shelter, and clothes...
God Good
Thankful that all of my needs...He knows...
God Good!

Oh taste and see that the Lord is good.
Psalm 34:8 NKJV

Prayers...

conversations between me and Him

BREATHE

Breathe into me O Lord

Comfort my soul

Refresh my mind dear Jesus, fill me…make me whole

Lord, cleanse my spirit and fill my heart with love

Let me rest in Your arms of safety

As you comfort me from above

Breathe into me O Lord, the breath of life

That I can be filled and made whole

And live life right

Breathe into me O Lord

Remove the pain from disappointment and strife.

Unless you breathe into me Lord, I have no life.

*And the Lord God formed man of the dust of the
ground, and breathed into his nostrils the breath
of life; and man became a living being.*

Genesis 2:7 NKJV

THIS IS MY PRAYER

Lord, let my life reflect Your goodness, mercy, and favor…
Lord, let my heart reflect Your Love…
Let my light shine that others might see You
Moving from up above
Let me feel Your hand of mercy, when I fall or go astray
Let me know Your forgiving power as
You restore me, this I pray
Let me be all You've called me to be,
as I walk in Your will today
Lead me…I'll follow. For You are the only Way.
Lord, let my praise be acceptable and
my walk match my praise…
Let me not succumb to status quo and
be hypocritical in my ways.
This is my prayer.

…I am the way, the truth, and the life. No one
comes to the Father except through Me.

John 14:6 NKJV

HIS WILL

As we go about our daily lives, we sometimes confuse our agenda with the Lord's will. Instead of asking God to come bless what we're doing, maybe we should go where God is blessing. Push!

In Your will is where I wanna be

Ultimately, Your face is the face I wanna see

My life Lord, I owe all to Thee

I want more of You and less of me

Hear me O Lord, accept my plea

Your grace, Your mercy, Your love has set me free

In You, my faith is planted…like a tree

In Your will is where I want to be

…more of You Lord, less of me.

Your will be done.
Matthew 6:10 NKJV

Life experiences not only result in growth (if the lesson is learned); but it also produces light that illuminates God's glory as He manifests Himself in the outcome.

Is your light shining?

Push…

I am the light of the world. He who follows me shall not walk in darkness, but have the light of life.

John 8:12 NKJV

YOUR LOVE

We are commanded to love others with the love of the Lord. God's love suffers for a long time, through all kinds of turmoil & challenges. His love rejoices in truth and accepts hardship and rejection. God's love is without special terms, conditions...there is no hidden agenda. His love is a selfless act that never fails. God's love is some kind of love...what kind of love are you giving?

Your love is

Amazing

Your love is

Unconditional

Your love is

Endless

Your love has

No Boundaries

Your love

Saves

Your love

Delivers

Your love

Set free

Your love

Gives life

Your love

Gives hope

Your love

Gives strength

O what love!

Love suffers long and is kind; love does not envy; love does not parade itself, is not puffed up; does not behave rudely, does not seek its own, is not provoked, thinks no evil; does not rejoice in iniquity, but rejoices in the truth; bears all things, believes all things, hopes all things, endures all things. Love never fails.

1 Corinthians 13:4-8a NKJV

AT HIS FEET

At His feet
I leave it there
All my burdens
He promised to bear
No longer bound
Shackled in defeat
I'm walking in victory
I left my cares at His feet.

…casting all your care upon Him, for He cares for you.
1 Peter 5:7 NKJV

DESPERATE FOR JESUS

In my darkest hour
Down, done in despair
I call on You Jesus
I know You're there

Can You hear me Lord?
Let me feel Your presence
I'm calling on You Jesus
Let Your spirit take residence

Savior, deliver me from myself
Can't walk, can't talk, can't make it with nobody else
I'm desperate for You Jesus
I'm desperate for You Jesus

On my knees
At Your feet
You promised me Lord
My hungry soul You'd keep

Now I seek Your face
As I call Your name
I heed Your Word
Standing unashamed

I need You Lord
Let me feel You Lord
Fill me Lord
I'm desperate for You Jesus
I'm desperate for You Jesus

Through my tears
In my pain
Storm after storm
Can't stand the rain

Omnipotent Power
Matchless King
Can't make it without Your Lord
You're my everything
I'm desperate for You Jesus
I'm desperate for You Jesus

The Lord, your God is with you, He is mighty to save.
Zephaniah 3:17a NIV

FILL ME UP LORD

Fill Me Up Lord
I am empty and in need
Fill me up Lord
You promised my hungry soul you'd feed
Fill me up Lord
I don't think I'll make it through the day
Fill me up Lord
I surrender, have Your way
Fill me up Lord
I won't give in
Fill me up Lord
Lord do it, again.

...It is written, Man shall not live by bread
alone, but by every word of God."

Luke 4:4 NKJV

DO I MAKE YOU PROUD?

Just as a child seeks validation from their
parents, Lord I seek to please You

My words and actions in accordance with Your will, heeding
to Your every instruction without any doubts and fears

Moving without questioning, exercising faith without examining,
not focusing on the facts, just moving forward by faith

When I strive to do my best, giving You my all-nothing less

Do I make You proud?

When I submit to You when my flesh desires otherwise…
standing firm on Your promises, no facades, no compromises

Do I make You proud?

Have I done all you've called me to do?

Is my praise pleasing to You?

Does my worship cause You to rise to Your feet?

Am I acting like a soldier in despair, in defeat?

Do my actions put a smile on Your face?

Am I growing weary from running this race?

Lord, do my thoughts move Your heart?

Do my words move us apart?

Does my attitude reflect You aloud?

Lord, I want to make You proud.

For we walk by faith, not by sight…Therefore we make it our
aim, whether present or absent, to be well pleasing to Him.
2 Corinthians 5: 7 & 9 NKJV

God's favor is abundant upon the obedient.
Push…

But without faith it is impossible to please him, for he who comes to God must believe that He is, and that He is a rewarder of those who diligently seek Him.

Hebrews 11:6 NKJV

BEND, DON'T BREAK

Tossed and turned by the winds of life
Your heart is filled with misery and strife
Dark, lonely filled with despair
Feeling empty, you need to fill His presence
To know He's really there
In and out, up and down
Trials you continue to face
Your faith test and tried
But don't compromise
Enter into the Holy Place
As you go through, what you must do
As you wonder, how much more to take
Stand, stand strong it can't last too long
Bend, but don't break.

Finally, my brethren, be strong in the Lord
and in the power of His might.
Ephesians 6:10 NKJV

GOOD FOR NOTHING

If we can't love one another with the love of Christ

Realizing we are not our own because He paid the price

If we can't speak a kind word to encourage
our sister or our brother

If we can't heed to the Scriptures and stop living undercover

If we can't help somebody and ignore
our own selfish ambitions

Offering our time and talents with no terms, no conditions

If we can't admonish our neighbor without passing judgment

Speaking no evil with a rude or negative comment

If we can't rejoice with our friends,
without malice or hypocrisy

Displaying no fake emotions, no
jealousy, no hidden animosity

If we can't be an example to our enemies
of God's love, mercy, and peace

If we can't lead someone to Christ, that they too can be free

If we can't live this life with purpose yielding to the King

We've missed the mark; we are in fact …good for nothing.

Let nothing be done through selfish ambition or conceit,
but in lowliness of mind let each esteem others better
than himself. Let each of you look out not only for his
own interests, but also for the interests of others.

Philippians 2:3-4 NKJV

REST IN HIM

Rest in him

Cast all your cares

Rest in Him

Seek His face, He's always there

Rest in Him

He is an Ark of Safety

Rest in Him

His promises are sure, never ever maybe

Rest in Him

He is a pillar of protection

Rest in Him

Experience His love, appreciate His affection

Rest in Him

Subject your thoughts, surrender your mind

Rest in Him

Rest assured, He's always on time.

*Be anxious for nothing, but in everything by prayer and
supplication, with thanksgiving, let your requests be made known
to God; and the peace of God, which surpasses all understanding
will guard your hearts and minds through Christ Jesus.*

Philippians 4: 6-7 NKJV

BEFORE I GO

Before I go, I want to leave my imprint on the world

I want to speak a word that heals, a word
that encourages, a word that moves

Before I go, I want to leave my imprint on the world

I want to help those in need, those who
are hungry, I want to feed

Before I go, I want to leave my imprint on the world

I want to fulfill God's purpose for my life; I
want to lead by example, live life right

Before I go, I want to leave my imprint on the world

It not enough just to live and to die, I want
to inspire others, teach them to fly.

…"What shall we do, that we may work the works of God?"
John 6:28 NKJV

YOU

From the pits of hell, You brought me

From guilt and shame, You delivered me

In perfect peace, You kept me

In times of trouble, You never left me

Lord, O Lord You are so good to me

My soul cries out to Thee

Lord, You are so worthy

Thank You; from my sin…You forgave me.

When I returned to You, You restored me

When I felt empty, You filled me

From the shackles of defeat, You freed me

From myself, You saved me

Lord, O Lord You are so good to me.

The Lord is my rock and my fortress and my deliverer;
My God, my strength, in whom I will trust;

Psalm 18:2 NKJV

THE LORD, MY LIFE

Without You Lord, I am an empty shell
My life is meaningless without You
I can't live, breath, move without You, Lord
If You remove Your hand from me, turn
Your face from me, I will die
I live because You live in me
I seek Your face for You are greater than anything
You are my Source, my all
Turn away…I will fall
I need You…can't live without your love
Lord, You are my life.

*He who has the Son has life; he who does not
have the Son of God does not have life.*

1 John 5:12 NKJV

EVEN ME

His grace is sufficient for me

His mercy is miraculous for me

His love abounds faithfully for me

His favor is accessible to me

His deliverance is available to me

His glory can be revealed to me

Although I am not worthy, His love is unconditional for me

His peace comforts me

His forgiveness includes me

His restoration covers me

His healing fixes me

His Kingdom includes me

Yes…even me.

…"My grace is sufficient for you, for My strength is made perfect in weakness."

2 Corinthians 12:9 NKJV

THE TURNING POINT

The turning point
The point of surrender and submission to His will
With a made up mind and determined spirit
His purpose you will fulfill

The turning point
The point of no return, no fears, no regrets
Walk by faith not by sight
Trust …your every need will be met

The turning point
The point of obedience, weary and tired
of running from your calling
Yield to His instruction, heed the lesson
He will keep you from falling

The turning point
The point of production, Yes to His will, Yes to His way
Hear His voice, act on His Word
Turn to Him today

The turning point
The point of correction, admit you don't know the way
Once lost now found and Heaven bound
Saved and delivered, you're now okay

The turning point
The point of compliance. Do right or do wrong
Your way or His way, make up your mind this day
Choose...you're waiting too long

The turning point
The point of relief. Rest in Him, that's a benefit
You chose to let go and now you know
The turning point...you've finally reached it.

...choose for yourselves this day whom you will serve...
Joshua 24:15 NKJV

LOST AND FOUND

How long must I wait and anticipate some
resolve to this test, this trial?

I know weeping only endures for a night,
but my night is lasting quite a while

How long must I wait not knowing my fate…
trying not to complicate this mess?

Trying to stand strong, it can't be too long, but
I can't have a testimony without a test

Woe is me, I cannot see my way out…
feeling trapped, feeling bound

Forgetting He paid the ultimate price
when His Son gave His life

Once lost, now I'm found.

*My brethren, count it all joy when you fall into various trials,
knowing that the testing of your faith produces patience.*

James 1:2-3 NKJV

It's so easy to get lost in the expectations of others, but our accountability to God is more important than an explanation to others.

Push...

Poetry...

words to enlighten, edify, and encourage

THE TITUS 2 WOMAN

She is…
A Woman of God
Woman of standard
Woman of integrity
Woman of candor
Woman of peace
Woman of truth
Woman of meekness
A woman like Ruth.
Woman of strength
Woman of humility
Woman of beauty
Woman of versatility
A woman of faith
A woman of power
A woman standards
Too strong to cower
Woman of love, joy, and peace
focused on His mission with a world to reach
That's who she is.

…the older women likewise, that they be reverent in behavior, not slanderers, not given to much wine, teachers of good things that they admonish the young women to love their husbands, to love their children, to be discreet, chaste, homemakers, good, obedient to their own husbands, that the word of God may not be blasphemed.

Titus 2:3-5 NKJV

PEOPLE PLEASING

People pleasing places pressure on pursuing the
personal expectations of the other person

Pleasing others results in a pause in the
cause that God prepared us for

Our pursuit should be to please God and God
alone; His plan should be our passion

People pleasing pleases no one. As we allow other people to make
their problems our priority, we pay the price as we permit others
to oppose what we know to be His perfect will for our lives

People pleasing prolongs the process as we ponder the
principles of His plan and pacify the people we aim to please

The approval from people pleasing pale in comparison to
the peace that passes all understanding if we apply that
same passion in the preparation to implement His plan

The people's perspective prevents the fulfillment of the promises
of God by persuading us to move outside of the blessed place

We must persist in performing His perfect will as
we seek His permission in every aspect of our lives.
We must be prayerful before proceeding

As partners in Christ, we possess the power for
great works and our possibilities are endless. Pray
and praise Him as we proclaim His power

Seeking Him passionately will make us less prone to promote the
petitions of other people, to whom we have nothing to prove.

But seek first the kingdom of God and His righteousness,
and all these things shall be added to you.

Matthew 6:33 NKJV

WORDS

Words do have power
Your response determines how much
Words can tear you down or build you up
And be felt as if a touch

Words do have power
So be mindful of how you use
Think before speaking
Of the power you're leaking
Your intent can leave a lasting bruise.

*Let no corrupt word proceed out of your mouth, but what is good
for necessary edification, that it may impart grace to the hearers.*
Ephesians 4:29 NKJV

FREE

I am who I am, just the way He created

Don't need bright lights or accolades, that
makes things too complicated

I am who I am, only by His grace

While I battle two natures and subject
to sin, still…I'm in a good place

I am who I am, no need to live a lie

Although I'm not perfect…far from
perfection…every day I try

I am who I am, striving to be who He called me to be

I can stand tall, with my integrity
intact, cause I'm free…totally.

Therefore if the Son makes you free, you shall be free indeed.
John 8:36 NKJV

MIND YOUR MIND

O you'd better mind your mind
Sittin idle, wastin time
Plottin, schemin
Wanderin, dreamin
Mind Your Mind

Too much time to do nothing
Work to be done, so do something
Mind Your Mind

What you take in, is what you give back
Good, bad, or ugly
It's a fact; your mind isn't so kind if you haven't
taken the time to mind your mind

The mind is a battlefield
Old nature versus the new
Mind your mind so you'll know what to do
When trouble comes, your mind won't
react to your flesh as you go through
Each trial you'll know to mind your mind so you can flow
In His will, surrender to His way,
please mind your mind today.

And do not be conformed to this world, but be transformed
by the renewing of your mind, that you may prove what
is that good and acceptable and perfect will of God.
Romans 12:2 NKJV

GOT TO GIVE IT UP

What are you willing to give up to get where you need to be?

What are you willing to sacrifice to be free in Him totally?

What are you willing to do without...
possessions or other material things?

You've got to give up those deadly treasures
so He can reign supreme.

Those things that bind us or distract us from our purpose...

Those things that separate us from Him
and leaves us feeling worthless...

Those things that shine and draw others attention...

Those thing that are unpleasant and
too shameful to mention...

You have to make a decision to live for Him today

Let no sin or stuff hinder you or stand your way

What are you willing to give up?

How important is your relationship with Christ?

In order to be who He wants you to be, you've got
to give it up or it could cost you your life!

*...if My people who are called by My name will humble themselves,
and pray and seek My face, and turn from their wicked ways, then I
will hear from heaven, and will forgive their sin and heal their land.*

2 Chronicles 7:14 NKJV

CHURCHIN'

There are too many celebrities in the church
when Jesus should be the only star

Sin more prevalent than the Word

Church, we've gone too far

How did we get it twisted, conflicted, confused?

Liars in the pulpit, hypocrites in the pews

Whatever happened to Jesus being the center of our joy?

Praise and worship means nothing now, it's merely a chore

Let us focus our hearts and long for the King

Repent and refrain from our lusts and
desires of fame and material things

Let's go back to our first love, remember
the moment you received Christ?

When He cleansed your heart, made you
whole, gave you a brand new life

Let's watch our walk and be mindful of our
words that our witness not be destroyed

There's a world to reach, a message to preach,
His Word will not return void.

*So shall my word be that goes forth from My
mouth; It shall not return to Me void*

Isaiah 55:11 NKJV

SENSE MAKE CHANGE

Sense make change while irrational
thinking can cause a mess

Sense brings about peace and helps you
make the decision that's best

Sense can bring calm to the most difficult situations

Sense eliminates turmoil and unnecessary aggravations

Sense can win others while conflict pushes them away

Sense reflects love and fruit you want to convey

Sense requires thought and consideration before action

Sense isn't selfish or based on personal satisfaction

Sense demands submission and surrender to His way

Sense make change, use your sense today.

Let this mind be in you which was also in Christ Jesus
Philippians 2:5 NKJV

TRUTH

It is what it is

No need to justify

Raw, plain, and simple

Let me testify

The Word stands alone

No explanation necessary

In Your heart the Truth

You must always carry

No room for misunderstanding, error, or a lie

Get it together now and tell it before you die

Live your life based on it

Speak words influenced by it

Teach your children how to tell it

Everyday walk in it

-Truth

And you shall know the truth and the truth shall make you free.
John 8:32 NKJV

WORK UNDONE

I'd rather live and be all that God has called
me to be, than die with my work undone.

Retakes or second chances after death…there are none.

When God calls me, I will answer…send me I will go.

A greater work to glorify the Kingdom, I just can't say no.

Approval from no one, trusting in Him and Him alone,

No time for uncertainty and doubts, or fear of the unknown.

I am chosen by Him; it's an honor to serve.

My service I can render, for His mercy
and grace, I don't deserve.

Praying that I will touch somebody while I'm on my way

Hear me O Lord; let me lead someone to You today.

I'd rather live and be all God has called me
to be, than die with my work undone.

So I shall live again, He'll welcome me
home and say servant well done.

…Well done, good and faithful servant;
Matthew 25:21 NKJV

PRICELESS

How much are you worth?

Child, do you know?

5, 10, 15, 20…how high should I go?

How much are you worth?

Proclaim your worth today

Is your worth far above rubies and diamonds
or are you too ashamed to say?

How much are you worth?

Have you been good to your temple?

Have you abused confused, misused…been just sinful?

How much are you worth?

Have you allowed words of destruction
and despair into your spirit?

Is it full of dirt, trash or other junk to deal with?

How much are you worth?

You need to decide today, that your worth isn't based
on outward appearances or the images you portray.

How much are you worth?

Realize you were fearfully and wonderfully made.

Your worth is far above worldly treasures…
a priceless amount of love He paid.

*Or do you not know that your body is the temple of the Holy
Spirit who is in you whom you have from God, and you not
your own? For you were brought at a price; therefore glorify
God in your body and in your spirit, which are God's.*

1 Corinthians 6:19 NKJV

RIPE TO RECEIVE

Are you ripe to receive?

Can you stand to be blessed?

Are your grumbling, mumbling, or complaining
as you go through your test?

Are you in position…where God wants you to be?

So He can bless you accordingly, and set you free…totally.

Are you holding fast to His promises,
standing firm in your faith?

He wants to bless you abundantly, but you must be in place.

Ready to receive every blessing He has is store…

Go ahead get in position before you ask for more.

Are you trusting in His Word?
Whose report will you believe?

Before He can truly bless you, you must be ripe to receive.

*And whatever we ask we receive from Him, because we keep His
commandments and do those things that are pleasing in His sight.*

1 John 3:22 NKJV

SEEDS

O be careful my sisters of the seeds you sow
The young daughters are watching you…don't you know?
Every word, every deed
Be responsible and take heed
O be careful my sisters of the seeds you sow
Integrity and strength of character are
traits you want to convey
It's not only what you do, but also what you say
Words like deeds have power, to tear down or build up
What message are you sending? Be honest, 'fess up.
It's time to be real and honest with yourself
Are you really you or are you trying to be someone else?
O be careful my sisters of the seeds you sow
The truth will set you free, act like you know
Our daughters are suffering while waiting on us to comply
Stand up, tell the truth, don't live a lie.

…the older women likewise, that they be reverent in behavior, not slanderers, not given to much wine, teachers of good things- that they admonish the young women to love their husbands, to love their children, to be discreet, chaste, homemakers, good obedient to their own husbands, that the word of God may not be blasphemed.

Titus 2:3-5 NKJV

CONFESS

Living like hell ain't real
Shackled with chains of defeat
Looking ragged, tattered, and torn
This life has you beat
Cast down from trials and tribulations
You're just barely getting by
Life doesn't have to be this way, let me tell you why
God has a purpose, a plan for your life
No need for suffering with misery and strife
Just surrender your will to His way
Open up your heart, let Him in today
Today can be the day of a new beginning, a new birth
Open your eyes and see what you're worth
You are precious and valuable in the Lord's sight
He wants your heart
Go ahead, give Him Your life.

...that if you confess with your mouth the Lord Jesus and believe in your heart that God has raised Him from the dead, you will be saved.

Romans 10:9 NKJV

GET IN POSITION

You can't be out of place and expect God to move
He's giving you instruction, what path will you choose?
Confused, no sense of direction, being
misled by fear and doubt,
You'd better get in position, stop that moving about
Stand still...take time to listen, yield your heart today
It's only when your surrender, He can have His way.

Stand still, and see the salvation of the Lord
Exodus 14:13 NKJV

IS IT I?

How many times do we find ourselves bound,
challenged, distracted, held back by IT?

Is IT I.. that keeps ME…from my purpose,
who YOU called ME to be?

I cannot understand why I am afraid of ME

I should be living with expectation;
You've already set ME free

I know I have a purpose; YOU equipped
ME when YOU called

I need to act on my faith with no focus on ME at all

I will live out my purpose, You've already set me free

It took a while but now I can finally be ME.

*Yet in all these things we are more than
conquerors through Him who loved us.*

Romans 8:37 NKJV

LOVE HIM

Love the husband God gave you
You've got a real good thing
Lord the husband God gave you
Remember the commitment and the ring?
Love the husband God gave you
Let no man come between
Love the husband God gave you
No hindrance or separation, that's what I mean,
Love the husband God gave you
He has flaws and so do you
Love the husband God gave you
Remember no one is perfect the next
time you're going through
Love the husband God gave you
At times it may seem hard to do
Love the husband God gave you
He chose him just for you.

Wives, submit to your own husbands, as to the Lord.
Ephesians 5:31 NKJV

TRUST

Have you ever second guessed God's instruction?

Can't think clearly cause you're trying to rationalize,
but you're slowing down your production

Have you ever questioned His reasoning?

Lord, why does it have to be this way?

Just know He knows what's best for us...that's all I can say

Have you ever requested confirmation for
His confirmation as if He was unclear?

Just activate your faith, stop operating in fear

Have you ever hesitated before acting on His Word?

As if you were unsure, of what He said or what you heard

Have you ever felt as if His decisions were unjust?

My friend I have to tell you all you have to do is trust.

*Trust in the Lord with all your heart, And lean not on
your own understand; In all your ways acknowledge
Him, And He shall direct your paths.*

Proverbs 3:5-6 NKJV

MEANING

A life defined by material things don't mean much

Collecting trinkets and do-dads, things that
depreciate in value...using them as a crutch

Where is the depth, our lives can mean so much more?

Why block your blessings and hinder the
flow God has so much more in store

Live each day with purpose and live
everyday as if it were your last

that you dare not live with regrets caught
singing the woes of your sinful past

Success in life cannot be measured by the items we
collect to display, but it is determined by the freedom
and peace of mind from yielding to His way.

*Do not lay up for yourselves treasures on earth, where moth
and rust destroy and where thieves break in and steal; but lay
up for yourselves treasures in heaven where neither moth
nor rust destroys and where thieves do not break in and steal.
For where your treasure is, there your heart will be also.*

Matthew 6:19-21 NKJV

Praise...

words of exaltation and adoration

MY GOD

My God is able to hear the desires of my
heart and fill my empty parts

He knows my every need; my hungry soul He feeds

He know me...my fingers, my toes, my hair, my nose

I am fearfully and wonderfully made

He chose me; He saved me, an awesome price He paid

He cares for me; He's always there for me

He calms my fears, He dries my tears

Grace and mercy He extends, on Him I know I can depend

Because of Him I can live free and be
all that He's called me to be

Life without Him would definitely be unkind

As good as My God is, who wouldn't serve a God like mine?

I will praise You, for I am fearfully and wonderfully made...
Psalm 139:14 NKJV

GRATEFUL

Every time I turn around, Your blessings over take me

Although I am not worthy, I must take time to thank Thee

Your grace and mercy are bountiful, for my
salvation You paid the ultimate price

Yes I'm grateful, but I must admit, I'm
not worthy of such a sacrifice

Lord, I'm grateful for Your love that showers me day to day

With a heart of gratitude, I will always say...

Thank You!

*I will bless the Lord at all times; His praise
shall continually be in my mouth.*

Psalm 34:1 NKJV

HE'S ABLE

My God is able to see the end from the beginning
and bring resolve to any situation

He meets all my needs, He feeds my soul,
He exceeds my expectations

He hears the desires of my heart, heals
my wounds, cleanses every part

He renews my spirit and calms my every fear

He lets me feel His presence just so I'll know He's near

He cares for me and protects me from all hurt and harm

He corrects me, chastises me, so to His will I conform

All knowing, all powerful, a mighty God I serve

His love is bountiful and has no limits,
most times I don't deserve

Gracious and merciful, a forgiving God is He

He is able and willing to be all that I need Him to be.
He's able…Yes, He is!

*Now to Him who is able to do exceedingly abundantly above all
that we ask or think, according to the power that works in us,*

Ephesians 3:20 NKJV

HE IS

...as good as a cool breeze on a hot summer day

...as good as the dew after a morning rain

...as good as a rainbow after a storm

...as good as the rhythm from your favorite song

...as good as the feeling of your greatest accomplishment

...as good as your most prized possession ever meant

...as good as the smile from your proudest moment

...as good as the goodness and mercy that you'll never forget

...as good as the relief from your most trying trial

...as good as the blessings from lessons
that make life worthwhile.

Praise the Lord, for the Lord is good
Psalm 135:3 NKJV

DON'T...

Don't be deceived by my beautiful smile or my
warm personality with no regard for my Creator

Don't misjudge my intentions without acknowledging
my Heart Regulator, my Motivator

Don't mistake my attitude of assurance with
the faith that I hold in someone greater

Don't confuse my strength with the
power that belongs to my Maker

Don't be misled by my words of wisdom
without considering the Author

Don't misinterpret my fearless attitude;
I have faith in my Father

Don't be misguided by my endurance as I embrace each trial

I don't walk alone; therefore I can walk for miles and miles.

*Looking unto Jesus, the author and finisher of our faith, who for
the joy that was set before Him endured the cross, despising the
shame, and has sat down at the right hand of the throne of God.*

Hebrews 12:2 NKJV

GOD'S SUPPLY

God's supply is so much more than what
our carnal minds can conceive

We've tried Him, we know Him…
yet sometimes we don't believe

God's supply is unlimited, it has no end

Our needs, He meets when placed at
His feet on Him we can depend

God's supply includes everything we need

The physical and the spiritual, our hungry souls He feeds

God's supply does not discriminate; it
doesn't matter where you're from

Trust in Him, Stand on His Word, He's calling You to come

God's supply is priceless, worth more than silver or gold

No money can amount to this awesome
gift, it includes riches untold

God's supply is matchless, there's none
like Him, He's The One.

He can do the impossible, reach the unreachable,
transform nothing into some.

*And my God shall supply all your need according
to His riches in glory by Christ Jesus.*

Philippians 4:19 NKJV

THE LITTLE THINGS

The breath I just took

Eyes to look

A voice to talk

Legs to walk

Ears to hear

Family that's near

Children that smile

Makes those nine months worth while

Wisdom and understanding

Yall betta hear me

Things aren't as bad as they could be

Time and time again, God of a second chance

Even when I've created the uncomfortable circumstance

Lord I thank You for giving me this day

Lord I thank You just for being the way.

*...in everything give thanks; for this is the
will of God in Christ Jesus for you.*
1 Thessalonians 5:18

THE IMPOSSIBLE

God can make the…
Unbelievable
Unfathomable
Invisible
Indescribable
Undeniable
Unreachable
Unattainable
Inoperable
Insurmountable
Inconsumable
Infeasible
Immeasurable
Irrefutable
Ineradicable
Impossible, Possible.

For with God nothing will be impossible.
Luke 1:37 NKJV

THE OUTCOME

In our darkest hour is sometimes where
we feel the most distance

We become paralyzed with fear and intimidated
by the night that surrounds us

The weight of the burden suppresses our efforts to pray

It's so hard to let go so He can have His way

The uncertainty of the outcome initiates uncontrollable
anxiety while undeniable fear obstructs our judgment

Faith cannot be found, all hope seems to be lost

Victory not yet declared, but the battle is already won.

...for the battle is not yours, but God's
2 Chronicles 20:15 NKJV

THAT

Yes, I did that that was me
I was guilty of that, until He set me free
Yes, I said that, until my tongue was bridled
I'm ashamed of that, when I put others before Him as idols
Now I am forgiven, no I won't look back
Cause God, as merciful as He is, has forgiven me for that.

*…if My people who are called by My name will humble themselves,
and pray and seek My face, and turn from their wicked ways, then I
will hear from heaven, and will forgive their sin and heal their land.*

2 Chronicles 7:14 NKJV

IT

IT's too big
IT's too hard
I can't do IT
IT can't happen
IT won't happen
I'm not good enough to do IT
I'm not qualified to do IT
IT's not possible, there's just no way
Whatever IT is, God can do IT!

Is there anything to hard for God?
Genesis 18:14 NKJV

THE ENCOUNTER

He touched, I felt…
He spoke, I heard…
He lifted, I rose…
He called, I answered…
He forgave, I'm restored…
He delivered, I'm set free…
He favors, I'm blessed…
He changed, I'm new…
He filled, I'm complete.

Therefore, if anyone is in Christ, he is a new creation; old things have passed away; behold, all things have become new.

2 Corinthians 5:17 NKJV

GO

Go beyond the thoughts that consume your
time and the uncertainty of your dreams

Go past the limitations of your mind
into the presence of the King

Go in with an humbled heart and allow Him full control

Go in with a heart of thanksgiving
and watch His glory unfold

Go where no man can take you, into the Holy Place

Go in, you will find Him waiting

Go, go today!

*Lord, who may abide in Your tabernacle? Who may dwell
in Your holy hill? He who walks uprightly, And works
righteousness, And speaks the truth in his heart*

Psalm 15: 1:2 NKJV

DESTINED

We cannot deny what God has destined to be
As soon as we accept Truth, is when we can clearly see
His purpose, His plan…no time for fear, just stand
On His promises, His Word is true
He will do just what He said He would do
Move in faith, leave no room for fear
God is with you, He's always near
His peace you'll experience as you walk in His will
Brighter days you'll see as His glory is revealed
Stay on the path of righteousness and you'll see…
The hand of God as you become all
that He's destined you to be.

Therefore humble yourselves under the mighty hand
of God, that He may exalt you in due time.

1Peter 5:6 NKJV

BECAUSE HE LOVES ME

He created me
Even in my mother's womb. He shaped me...
Just as He would have me to be, He molded me...
He created me...
Because He loves me

He chose me
Even in my sin, He forgives me...
Extending grace and mercy, He is just you see...
He chose me...
Because He loves me

He protects me
Even from danger I can't see, He cares for me...
On Him I can depend, He's faithful to me...
He protects me...Because He loves me

He provides for me, He supplies all my needs...
He fights for me, Hears my every plea...
He provides for me...
Because He loves me

He loves me.
He gave His only Son to die for me...
Although I am not worthy He still freed me...

When He chose me…
Because His loves me.

Greater love has no one than this, than to lay down one's life for his friends.

John 15:13 NKJV

GIVE BIRTH

Push…No matter how big the circumstance, God is greater than your issue. It is His will for you to succeed. He only wants the best for you. As a believer, you have the power to overcome that which seeks to destroy you and hinder you from your purpose. The Word declares that we are more than conquerors…more than conquerors! You are strong. You are equipped. You can do it! While trials will come, rest assured that He can, He will fulfill His promises. Your faith is the foundation for your calling. In order to produce greater works, surrender and trust Him today. Push past the pain from previous disappointments and give birth to something greater…your purpose!

Push…

When you allow your words to come alive in your spirit, then you can move beyond the uncertainty of the possibility into the realm of reality.

Push…

I press toward the goal for the prize of the upward call of God in Christ Jesus.

Philippians 3:14 NKJV

ABOUT THE AUTHOR

Alicia is a young woman who has discovered her life's purpose: to encourage, empower, and enlighten others with the written word. Her personal story is one that includes struggles with self esteem, fear of failure, and bondage from the opinions of "people", yet she overcomes by faith pushing past the pain from previous disappointments and gives birth to something greater...her purpose.

Alicia began public speaking while enrolled at the University of West Florida. Since then, she has participated at various conferences, workshops, and churches. Her mission is to share the love of Christ with as many people as she can reach and warm the hearts of each spirit she encounters as she encourages ..."the push".

Alicia lives in Florida with her husband and children. She loves traveling, writing, reading, and shopping.

For booking or more information about Alicia Waters:
Alicia Waters
1765 E Nine Mile Road Suite 1 #285
Pensacola, FL 32514
info@watersword.net
www.watersword.net
www.aliciawaters.com